OUT-FIGHTING
Long Range Boxing

The Deluxe Edition

Jim Driscoll

Featherweight Champion of the World

PROMETHEAN PRESS

Out-Fighting: Deluxe Edition

Promethean Press
1846 Rosemeade Pkwy #192
Carrollton, TX 75007
www.promethean-press.com

Copyright © 2008 by Promethean Press

All rights reserved, including the right of reproduction in whole or in part in any form.

Foreword taken from the book,
My Fighting Life, by Georges Carpentier.
Cassell and Company, 1920.

"Remembering Jem Driscoll" adapted from the book,
Knuckles and Gloves by Bohun Lynch.
W. Collins Sons & Co., 1922.

Manufactured in the United States of America

ISBN 978-0-9737698-4-5

TABLE OF CONTENTS

Foreword   **1**
Preface   **3**

Chapter One: Is It Obsolete?   **5**
Chapter Two: Long-Range Boxing As It Should Be   **19**
Chapter Three: Out-fighting On Equal Terms   **35**
Chapter Four: The Walking-In or Stand-Up Opponent   **47**
Chapter Five: Some Important Points to Be Observed   **61**

Addendum: Driscoll Beats Baldwin   **73**
            Remembering Jem Driscoll   **77**

FOREWORD

Jim Driscoll I shall always consider to have been one of the greatest of champions. It was not my good fortune to see him at his best, but even now there is no such stylist, no more perfect model of a boxer in all the countries. It is sometimes said that a boxer can scarcely hope to achieve greatness if he has unusual imagination. Driscoll destroys any such supposition. He has all the fire of his race; his brain is all life and sparkle; his eyes are all light and brightness; his form is a classical form; his face bespeaks high intelligence. Driscoll was never a fighter in the popular sense; he was, and even in the winter of his boxing days is, a wonderful man of boxing science.

He has been described as the personification of the English school; but not the English school as it is today, for its members are given to running before they can walk. They are not deep-thinking students; they have never been taught as Driscoll was taught. Charles Ledoux has told me that never has he been so belittled as he was by Driscoll.

This Ledoux, the majority of the critics say, is no boxer just a slogger. Ledoux can and does box cleverly, but not like Driscoll. Driscoll was the king of all boxers. From Driscoll, by a close study of his ways, I learned the wisdom of always leading with the left hand; he taught me much about stance, and how to time my blows so that they would have all the weight of my body behind them. What a different fighter Pal Moore, the American bantam, would be if he had been taught and trained by Driscoll.

Georges Carpentier

PREFACE

JIM DRISCOLL, the incomparable, was born at Cardiff in 1881, and began his boxing career in 1901 with nine fights, nine victories - seven of the latter by the knockout. His first appearance at headquarters was in 1904, when he met and defeated Boss Edwards. In 1908 he visited America, where, among others, he beat Charlie Griffin, Matty Baldwin, and Grover Hayes.

CHAPTER ONE
IS IT OBSOLETE?

If we are to listen to all the expert critics who are so anxious to tell the men who do the work how they ought to do it, we ought, I suppose, to at once cut out every brand of boxing except the in-fighting department. Our advisers keep on telling us that we are being beaten by our American and French rivals simply and solely because we have neglected in the past, and persist in neglecting in the present, the careful study of in-fighting. Which is to say, I suppose, because a few of us here and there have steadily refused to have anything to do with the holding, hugging, wrestling and roughing business, that we have been the principal cause of the decline, decay and ruin of English boxing. At least, I suppose that that is what they mean. For they scarcely ever have a word to say about any falling off in our out-fighting. They altogether ignore the fact that in the old days, when this modern roughing, wrestling business was unknown, and would never have been permitted if it had been known, English boxers could practically hold their own with those of any other country.

Perhaps they have become converts to an American belief (at all events, I have seen the statement in an American paper and over the signature of a well-known American sporting writer) that the old upstanding English or classic style is as dead as mutton. And yet, I dare swear that scarcely one of them - if indeed any of these generous or scientific advisers have ever witnessed a bout between a really tiptop, well-trained (don't forget the well-trained) exponent of the classic style and a champion of the rushing and hugging order, on the all-in, take-as-it-comes lines. I could not quote a single instance when a really great out-fighter has been beaten on his merits by even the greatest in-fighter ever known. I am disposed to fancy that if they had been present at a few contests, which I could mention, they would not be so cocksure then that the days of out-fighting had gone forever and would never return.

It would be interesting to know what the public think about

it all, or rather what they would think if they would only take the trouble to do some hard thinking. So far as I can see, they appear inclined to follow the line of argument pointed out for them. They have been told that in-fighting is the real winning suit, and, as support for the contention, they have had their attention drawn to the repeated victories of French and American boxers over Englishmen. The critics are careful to keep an absolute silence about any English triumphs won at the expense of the representatives of other countries, and they also omit to throw out any remarks on the possible absence of in-fighting altogether from the contests to which they draw attention. Because you know, or ought to know if you don't, that quite a number of these English defeats are not due to any lack of familiarity with in-fighting at all. Or, perhaps, that isn't the right way to put it: what I mean is, that our men have been beaten at every department of the game.

They have been beaten at out-fighting as well as at in-fighting. They have been beaten at punching, and they have been beaten at taking punches. And they have been beaten, worst of all, at staying power, speed and everything else which a man is supposed to cultivate in training. Our boys don't train, and that is really the cause of all the trouble. At least, only a few of our boys train as they ought to do.

Look at some of the Welsh boys, for instance. Percy Jones, Llew Edwards and Jimmy Wilde, to mention only three names, are able to win their matches. You don't hear of them being beaten, do you? No, of course you don't. And I don't remember to have heard that they have won their battles because they are so wonderfully adept at in-fighting. At least, I haven't noticed any remarks to that effect. No, the boys win because they know how to box, and because they have all worked hard to develop their ability; and also, and by no means least importantly, because they all train hard and conscientiously.

The French boys have come along so fast of late years for the very simple reason that they have all taken to the game

PREPARED TO HOOK WITH THE LEFT
Note that the right hand is ready to either stop a left lead to the face or to push down a body blow.

so seriously. They all meant to get to the top of the tree if they could, and they have got there. They started at the beginning, or rather, in most cases, earlier than the beginning, and they have kept right along. They don't smoke, they don't drink, and they don't dissipate in any way. Consequently, they come into the ring as fit as the proverbial fiddle, are able to cut out a tremendous pace and to keep it up, right through twenty rounds if necessary.

Watch a French boy going through a bad time. Let him get a hard punch, which puts him down for a long count. Say he gets up again, wobbling and weak. He may be badly shaken and, to all appearances, "all in." Say he gets a bad hammering and is put down again perhaps half a dozen times. You expect the towel to go in at any moment, but you don't see it. He goes down and gets up. He is thumped from pillar to post, but he struggles on, and all the time he is saving himself and pulling himself round until, finally, when the next round comes along, or it may be even a round or two later, still you will see him prancing around and holding his own, almost as fit and well as he was when he started. Now a man has to look after himself really well to be able to do that. He has to work hard and conscientiously on the road and in the gym, and he has got to take the very greatest possible care of himself in private life.

That is the reason why the French boxers have succeeded, and it is the only reason, or at all events the chief one. Add to this the fact that the French boxers are, as a rule, better educated and more intelligent than our men; that they think more, that they think harder and that they study their profession more intelligently and more conscientiously, and you can cut out all the in-fighting explanations.

The Americans succeed for precisely similar reasons. They, too, are better educated and are mostly more intelligent than the general run of our boys, and they one and all live much more cleanly and carefully, besides which they all train much harder and more scientifically. It isn't a difference

French boxer Georges Carpentier in action.

of method at all. It is a difference of material.

We shall never succeed in putting English boxers and boxing back where they belong unless we follow the same plan. We must catch our boxers young. We shall have to catch a better class of man. We shan't, by the way, have so much difficulty in doing this last, because it seems to me that the boys who are growing up today are, as a rule, all better educated and more intelligent than their parents.

And then we shall have to make them train. A good few of them won't like training in the least, especially if they are made to work hard, because a really hard spell of training is about the hardest work anyone can find anywhere. Where the boys will find it comes hardest will be in the constant training. For they have got to be always at it, if they mean to succeed. All right - I know what you are going to say, viz., that I never used to keep myself in constant training and that I did all sorts of other things which don't agree with any of the pre-

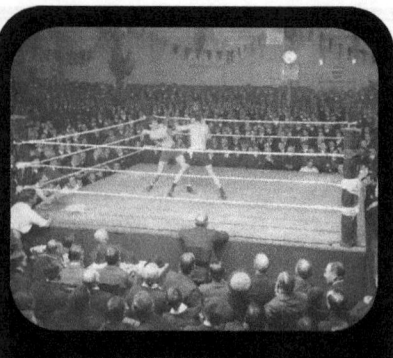

JEM DRISCOLL LOSES FIGHT FOR FOULING

English Featherweight Butted Welsh Repeatedly with His Head and is Disqualified

New York Times
December 21, 1910

CARDIFF, Wales. Dec. 20. - Freddie Welsh, the lightweight champion of England, won his fight with Jem Driscoll, the featherweight champion, in the tenth round tonight on a foul.

The fight was a twenty-round match for a purse of $12,500, the largest ever put up in Great Britain for little men. A crowd of several thousand witnessed the go, and, notwithstanding the fact that the betting favored Welsh, the spectators were greatly disappointed when the contest came to an unexpected end, due to Driscoll butting his opponent under the chin with his head.

Welsh, besides being five years younger than Driscoll, had the advantage of weight and reach. His blows were heavier than those of the featherweight champion, and cepts I am laying down. But I am telling you what I tell the boys in Wales: "Do as I tell you to do; don't do as I did, or as I am doing now, for that matter. I had my fling in my time, but if I were to have my time all over again you would see a very different Jim Driscoll. I won and kept on winning in spite of myself, not because my way of life was the best. You can try and explain this as you like, if you care to do so, but you will never get me to agree that any other boy in the future is going to be as successful as I was, if he proposes to live in the same way as I lived and to take as little care of himself as I used to do. It was luck and not judgment in my case. And of course I had to pay for it all. I can look back now on my training experiences during the last few years that I was an active member of the ring, and you can bet that they were awfully like purgatory. Anyway, I hope purgatory isn't going to be any worse. I should have had a better time of it when I was trying to get myself fit for Fred Welsh, for my second American trip, for my first contest with Spike Robson, and for my last two battles with Poesy and Owen Moran, if I had been a wiser and a better boy in my earlier years."

Why, they used to howl at me in the States. I remember on my first trip how they all used to stare when they saw me smoking cigarettes and drinking beer after each of my fights. All the American boys went straight back to their training camps after each fight and settled down to train again. Of course they all took an easy every now and then, but, as a rule, it was train, fight, train, fight, all the time with them.

I remember poor Stanley Ketchel coming up to me and asking how much I paid the Pressmen to keep them from slating me. He could scarcely believe me when I told him that I had never dropped a dollar to any of the sporting writers. "Why," he said, "if I went on out of the ring and between fights in the same way that you do the Press would just raise such a howl that you'd never get your hearing back. They're pretty hot on

he showed that he was able to take more punishment.

In the first round Driscoll had the advantage in points, but in the second Welsh landed several hard blows, and in that and the next round his extra weight, ten pounds, began to tell. In the fourth Welsh sent Driscoll to his knees, and the betting went from 2 to 1 to 5 to 1 in his favor.

The lightweight champion inflicted several damaging kidney punches in the seventh, but in the next round Driscoll got home a couple of hard straight leads that drew great applause. He followed this up with a great exhibition throughout the ninth, honors being even in that round on points. It was seen in the tenth, however, that Driscoll was fast tiring. His arms were hanging listless part of the time, his blows lack steam, and he clung to his opponent at every opportunity. In one of the clinches he persistently butted his opponent, and the referee finally disqualified him.

Welsh was loudly hooted in the sixth and seventh rounds for using the kidney punch so often. Driscoll was cautioned for butting in the seventh and in the tenth rounds. Getting his head under his opponent's chin, he butted Welsh badly, pushing him all around the ring. Then the referee separated them.

High words arose among the seconds and a free fight began, while Driscoll, badly cut up, stood with tears streaming down his face. Driscoll was the popular favorite, and the spectators expressed loud and long disapproval of the result.

me now as it is. They all accuse me of doping (*i.e.*, taking drugs) just because I drink a glass or two of beer every now and then, but I don't drink half or a quarter as much as you do." And it was true. He didn't. It was also true that they were always picking at him.

Now just keep an eye on these boys, Percy, Llew, and Jimmy. They don't drink and they don't smoke. They all live quietly and look after themselves. I'd give them a rare old tanning if any of them broke loose. But they won't. They are wise boys, all of them, and they know how to behave. What is more, they haven't any inclination to break loose. And that's why they all win, and it's also why, barring accidents, they're all going to be champions of the world one of these days. If we could only find a few good big fellows of the same stamp down in Wales, you wouldn't hear so much about the decadence of British boxing, or about its all being due to our national neglect to study the American style of in-fighting.

I was wondering just now what the public thought about it all, but I know without wanting anyone to tell me what they would think if the boxers were to listen to the preachers and critics. Supposing they all started in tomorrow to study in-fighting, without troubling in the least (as they wouldn't trouble) about training hard or about altering their mode of life. Just think what the contests would be like, especially if they were being handled by some of the referees I could name. A good lot of our boxing contests are bad enough now, as it is, but what they would be like *then*, I leave you to guess. For one thing, it would be the end of the game as far as this country was concerned, because the public would never stand for it at all.

No, the men who are making a fetish at in fighting, and who are advising us all to make it our most careful study and practice, simply don't know what they are talking and writing about, and haven't troubled to think about it either. They heard (someone told them, I suppose), that some French or American fighter had beaten some English fighter at in-fight-

Llew Edwards and Jim Driscoll

ing, and that the thing had happened lmore than once, and this was quite enough for them. They had to find some sort of explanation for these defeats, and it seemed to them that they had one right there. So they got busy on it.

I suppose it has never occurred to them that every boxing contest must necessarily start as an out-fighting exchange, and that every single round of every contest must also start that way. The men start from opposite corners of the ring and must get close together before any in-fighting can take place. For which reason it naturally follows that every man who has ever been beaten at in-fighting must necessarily have first been beaten at out-fighting, and that before they (the eloquent writers) start abusing us for our neglect to study in-fighting, they might more profitably devote a few hours' labour to a discussion on the decay of our long-range boxing, and, in conclusion, explain to us that we are no longer occupying the first, or even the second place as a boxing nation for the simple reason that we have forgotten how to box at long range, and that we have neglected the practice of it for the sake of developing our in-fighting, without taking the trouble to train properly for either. I should be right with them there.

No, out-fighting (*i.e.*, long-range boxing) is by no means obsolete. It isn't practised, it isn't studied, and it isn't cultivated. Scarcely any of our boxers train on the right lines, and hardly any single one of them trains either hard or conscientiously. There you have the real secret of the whole trouble.

Having slipped your opponent's left lead, you can send your right to his jaw as he flounders past you.

CHAPTER TWO
LONG-RANGE BOXING AS IT SHOULD BE

It isn't particularly easy to define out-fighting. The difficulty arises chiefly from the differences of opinion which exist about it. So few people can agree as to where out-fighting stops and in-fighting begins. So, for the purposes of my argument, I propose to assume that out-fighting is all boxing which takes place when two men are not actually in holds. That is to say, when either can jump back if he so wills, without having to tear himself loose from his opponent. So long as each man has both arms free, one can scarcely describe the exchanges as being anything else than out-fighting, because the range will shift about so rapidly.

There is, however, one form of out-fighting which is specially worthy of consideration, if only because it is the most effective and successful method of stopping the inveterate in-fighter from getting in close. In the old days, say, from fifteen to twenty years ago, or even more recently than that, when two men got close together, they would usually proceed to at once fight themselves free. They might come close in their excitement - one might almost say in their fury. They may "not have wanted to get close, but they used to get there, and then we used to see a quick, sharp, short spell of hard double-handed hitting before both retreated to long range and returned to pretty, scientific, open boxing. It was yery clever, perhaps, and it was certainly far prettier as a spectacle, but I am not at all sure that the modern school of fighters are not correct, when they assert that it was neither as strenuous, as hard, nor even as clever as the modern style. For one has to acknowledge that a good deal of the present-day in-fighting is really wonderfully clever and. tricky. One has only to watch such men as Fred Welsh in action to realise how very clever and tricky it can be. The blocks, the clever way in which an opponent's arm is trapped, the swift, sharp back-handers, the little jabs, jolts and upper cuts, the sharp snappy punches, which, even if they are not particularly heavy, and even if they don't hurt, yet succeed in piling up points, must all have been carefully thought out and practised.

I can well understand how the average man watching all this might come to the conclusion that here was the real, the only sure winning game. That is provided the same average man had not paused to reflect that, in order to get in close and to do all this execution, the man must continue to get past the left hand and the out-fighting of his opponent. Now it is all very well to assert that the in-fighter has proved the superiority of his method simply because he has got past and worked in close, but, as a matter of fact, he hasn't proved anything of the kind. All that he has proved is that he is himself a clever tactician and that his opponent is either a poor tactician or else a poor out-fighter. That is really all that has happened.

Remember that we did not see Welsh get in close to McFarland. For one thing we did not even see him try to do so until towards the end of their contest at the N.S.C. Well, yes, Freddie did perhaps make several dashes to get in, but you can't say that they succeeded or that he was able to do anything of particular note when he did get inside. This wasn't because Packey was able to beat him at in-fighting, but simply because Packey wasn't having any. The Chicago boy is a great out-fighter, perhaps one of the very best long-range boxers in ring history, and he meant to make the contest a long-range battle. He kept his left hand going most of the time, and he kept it going so fast and so accurately that Freddie could only rarely get past it, and when he did he only got uppercut by Packey's right for his pains.

Matt Wells had a somewhat similar experience when he met MacFarland in New York. Matt rushed for all he was worth. He kept up a continual series of charges, but he gained very little by so doing. Packey was always busy, and if there wasn't a vast amount of punishment on either side during those 10 rounds, well, Matt can never be said to have really succeeded in either getting home hard on Packey, or in getting to close quarters.

Then take Jimmy Wilde. How often do you see anyone

The Jim Driscoll-Freddie Welsh contest. Shaping for action.

succeed in scoring in a spell of in-fighting with little Jimmy? And how often do you see Jimmy trying to do any in-fighting on the American plan himself? You could answer "Never" to both questions, and the exceptions would be so rare, even if there have been any, that your answer would be quite correct. Yet Wilde is invariably sent up against men who are pounds heavier, sometimes more than a stone heavier. His opponents are taller, longer in the reach and stronger than he is. Some of them are quite clever in-fighters. And whatever you do, you must not forget that Jimmy has to keep close, as close as he can, as otherwise he might not be able to reach his men. Yet these fellows don't clinch. They are not able to score at the in-fighting game, for the simple reasons that Jimmy won't let them in the first place and, in the second, because he is such a clever out-fighter that they can't get "in," no matter how hard they try.

One has only to remember these things, to think them over, to realise that the in-fighter can never get his work in, if the out-fighter only knows his business and can punch hard enough. Don't forget that last bit, by the way. Because any in-fighter - any close-quarter man, that is - must be as strong and rugged as they are made, and must be in thorough training if he is going to make good. The chief reason for the in-fighters' success has been that they have generally succeeded in wearing their opponents down. That is what they aim at doing. That and the ability to stand more punishment than the other fellow can give them. Of course a superb defensive fighter like Welsh does not look for punishment, but then he is a fighter of a unique kind, one of a special stamp, in a class all by himself in that he is careful to avoid receiving any more punishment than he can help and also doesn't rely to any extent on beating an opponent up.

In fact, one may say that Welsh's most dangerous and damaging punch is his kidney punch, and those who watch him carefully have noticed that Freddie's kidney punch isn't the sort of thing which should have been permitted even when kidney punching was legal in England. It goes in America all right, of course, but then - over there - there are numerous punches and methods of punching to which no one objects, each and all of which are foul according to the strict letter and spirit of our rules.

There used to be, and still is, an idea that no English boxer can become a really first-class man until he has been through an American tour. There is something to be said for the idea, although the conclusion is all wrong. This conclusion is that an American experience improves a man's boxing and enables him to learn a lot of things which he could not possibly pick up on this side. I have even heard the argument advanced as affording proof positive that the Americans are ahead of us at the boxing game, and have also heard it supported by the further contention that the rapid progress of boxing across the English Channel is solely due to the fact

BREAKING FROM AN OPPONENT WHO CLINCHES PERSISTENTLY

Push opponent back with your left, so that you can drive a right upper cut to the chin, press his head back with this and thus force him to loosen his hold.

that the best and most successful coaches in France were all Americans. It is even claimed that the French style was American in its origin (which is more or less correct) and that it is still mainly American (which it isn't). The French style, if it is anything, is rather a blend of the English and American schools.

But there is one thing which the English visitor to America learns, which he has to learn if he is going to do any good over there - and that is training. A man who doesn't know how to train or who trains only on the average modern English lines, would never have a chance of making good in the States. He would never be able to stay the pace for one thing, and he wouldn't be able to stand the pounding for another.

Yet I cannot say that America taught me anything in the boxing line. They didn't even teach me how to train. Perhaps if I had been several years younger and had been dreaming dreams of a great future career, I might have been induced to alter my methods and to keep myself fit between bouts. I saw the wisdom of their methods, but I was too old and too fixed in my habits to change, and anyway, I believe that I had realised it all before.

No, I cannot say that America taught me anything much. In fact, if there was any instruction imparted, I am inclined to fancy that I did the instructing, and I was neither the first nor the last English boxer who has put the Americans up to a few wrinkles.

One thing they didn't understand was, how I contrived to outpace them. They could see that I was living on a wrong plan entirely. They noticed that I didn't rush back into training as soon as I was through with a bout. They knew that I was wrong and that they were right, and yet they could neither travel at the pace I set nor could they keep it up. Can you wonder that they were badly puzzled? You may be puzzled as well, by the way, if you are going to try to reconcile this statement with my previous one, that no boxer who is content to train on the average modern English lines can hope to stay

American heavyweight champion Jack Johnson

the pace of a Philadelphian six-rounder. And yet the explanation is quite a simple one.

For the American tears in for all he is worth. He pounds away with all his might, hit or miss, and he wastes or can be made to waste a large percentage of his punches. He is always trying so desperately to get close up where he can hurt you, and he is also hoping so fervently that he will succeed in sending you down for the full count, that he is comparatively easy to hit. That is if you really and truly understand good long-range fighting. And if you do really and truly understand that, he isn't at all difficult to avoid. But one needs to be armed with a good accurate left hand which carries a good deal of powder behind it, and one also needs to be quick and active on one's feet.

You see the American method has all the defects of its qualities. The American fighter is trained to go right into a man and mix things. He has been brought up to expect that the opponents he is likely to meet will either come to meet him with exactly similar intentions and on exactly similar lines, or else that they won't be able to either avoid or resist his attack. So some of them come rushing in like furious rams, almost as though they had been fired from a gun, or else they walk in as poor Harry Lewis used to do. In either case they are prepared and anxious to hit fiercely and furiously as hard as they can from every and any angle and to keep on hitting all the time.

Those of you who saw poor Harry Lewis in action in this country and in France will remember that he wasn't very difficult to hit. It is true that he was well practised in the knack of dropping his head forward a little so that he could take one's straight punches on the forehead or on the top of the head, but it wasn't necessary to aim your blows there, nor was he always successful in taking all the punches aimed at him in one or other of those spots. Where Lewis really shone and where his best asset lay was in the peculiar bony shape of his head, which enabled him to laugh at punches on the jaw and face which would have sent most other men down on the floor for keeps.

In fact, I am rather inclined to suspect that he overdid things in this respect. I shouldn't be at all surprised to learn that his final collapse and present paralysis was due quite as much to his habit of persistently sticking out his jaw as an open target and to the frequent terrific punches he took there-

Bombardier Wells is stopping one of Gunner Moir's rushes with a right to the face.

on, as to the after-effects of the cab accident. Both were contributory causes, I expect, for no man can expect to have his head punched so frequently and so hard as poor Harry used to positively ask his opponents to punch him, without feeling the effects or without one day having to pay the bill.

Yet Lewis and other rugged American fighters of the same stamp usually walk in in this fashion; asking to be hit and content to be hit, because they feel confident that they will get in close in time, to hand over a few winning punches which will put the other fellow down and out.

They have done this sort of thing scores of times against English and French rivals, and have done it with full and complete success, for the simple reason that they have felt an absolute contempt both for the hitting power of those rivals and for their ability to stand punishment. I can't say what sentiments they have about their opponent's footwork, but if they had or have any at all they must be ones which are immeasurably below contempt.

For it is the absolute lack of anything approaching even decent footwork which has made our men such an easy prey for the American sloggers. Our fellows have simply stood still to receive the onslaught. Sometimes they have merely collapsed in front of it and when they haven't done that they have tried to swap punches, without possessing either the necessary, receptive powers and without having gone through the training necessary either to strengthen their frames or to infuse sufficient punching power into their own wallops. To put the thing concisely, they have tried to fight the Americans at their own game without having even the glimmering of an idea how to do it.

Yet even the toughest of these sloggers should be fairly easy to beat, if one only cares to go the right way about it. The correct method is to refuse to mix things with them, to make a judicious use of the ring and to keep them at long range. One has to be in good and sound training for the purpose and one also has to be able to punch hard and sharply.

Never let them get their double-handed punching into working order. Stab them as they come in, send your fist sharply and crisply to their faces and then, if you haven't checked their advance, get away before they can retaliate. If

PENETRATING A SMOTHER

Pushing a smothered-up opponent aside and sending the right to his ribs.

you have given them a check, repeat the stab, and cross your right if you are sure of the opening. And if you can't get away, well, just step in and claim their arms. There is no necessity to hold them. It is as well to be careful on this score, because they are quite capable and are quite strong enough to tear either one or both arms free and to make you regret having come into holds. In no case consent to any in-fighting spell. You have little to gain by one, while they have everything. Be content to trap their arms with your gloves, to push them back and then jump away.

Always get away for preference, because if you are at all smart on your feet and if you have a fast, an accurate and an even decently respectable left-hand punch, you are going to score points fast and you are going to shake them up pretty considerably. They will come on and keep coming on, but if you get home and keep on getting home and also keep on getting away, you are going to rattle them and also to break down their strength, more than a trifle, in time.

Best of all, perhaps, you are going to annoy them. You will, after a while, make them so vexed that they will start to rush at you. You will need to be especially quick and lively then, because those rushes will always be dangerous. But if you have trained and practised on the right lines, you should be able to side-step even all their most furious rushes, without any overwhelming difficulty, and then as you side-step you can knock their blows aside, step in and cross, hook or jab them as they flounder past, and at the close of every round experience the satisfaction of knowing that you have advanced another stride towards victory.

I have sketched out this plan on the assumption that you are, firstly, by no means too sure of your powers, and secondly, that you are liable to be not too strong in defence and quite possibly somewhat inferior in strength. You are also extremely likely to be inferior both in the ability to take punishment and also to some extent in the pace of your hitting from various angles. You *must not* be slower on your feet and you must not be slower in your straight punching. For if you are slower in either of these departments you are going down to defeat somewhat speedily.

CHAPTER THREE
OUT-FIGHTING ON EQUAL TERMS

Let us assume, for the sake of argument, that you are up against a determined and most aggressive in-fighter - a man who is more rugged than you are and also a man who can, as a rule, not only punch much harder but also much faster when you allow him the chance to get in as close as he likes to do.

Say, for instance, that this man makes a practice of rushing at you. Well, let him rush, but don't wait to meet his rushes. For that way madness and quite possibly disaster lies. This is the stamp of man who can best be beaten by making him beat himself. Coax him to come at you. Dodge him, slip him. Let him loose his fiercest, wildest, and heaviest swings. For very nearly all these men are swingers, first, last and all the time, and pretty hefty swingers at that. A good few of them even, as they themselves put it, pick their punches right up from the floor.

Since they are so strong and such powerful punchers, however, it isn't safe to take chances with them. Nor is it at all necessary. They are apt to fling themselves at you, and, consequently, they are liable to strain and badly tire themselves when they find their aim has gone astray. Nothing tires a man so much as to miss and to keep on missing. For you must not forget that if a fighter of this stamp has gained any really big reputation, he hasn't been in the habit of missing, and so he will soon get both mentally and physically distressed.

Again, since he doesn't in the least mind - prefers, in fact, to put pretty nearly all his force and weight into every punch he sends out, it stands to reason that he is accustomed to travel at a certain particular pace and will not be able to stand the double strain of both lashing out with all his force and vigour and of also traveling considerably faster than usual for long. He will continue to hit out as hard as he can for as long as he can, because that has become almost a second nature with him, and it is up to you to see that he keeps on traveling above his usual pace for as long as you can make him, because the longer he does both, the quicker he is going to

SENDING HOME A RIGHT COUNTER

Sending home a right counter to the ribs after having drawn a left lead.

collapse.

Elsewhere [in the book *Ringcraft*], I have laid particular stress on the fact that nothing exhausts a man quicker or more readily than to be forced to travel faster than his usual wont, and that it is by no means impossible to have a man stretched out gasping and helpless on the floor, while the full count is called over him, without having put yourself to the exertion of sending in a knock-out punch, either to the jaw or mark. It is, of course, safer and wiser to send the punch across all the same, because it is always unwise to assume that you have won a boxing match before you have actually done so. But it isn't particularly difficult to force a man out of his usual gait, to make him spurt and to keep him spurting.

Say that you have been content to dodge his first onslaught and that you have either jabbed him as he went past or have allowed him to thunder by unharmed. On the other hand, you may, perhaps, have seen a chance to plant home a sharp left to the face before the rush was made. But in either case it is advisable to slip the first few charges. Don't make the mistake of slipping them too easily. Be careful to convey the impression that you escape more by luck than judgment. Never wander too far away. Keep circling round. Stab home a left, even plant a right dig, if you are perfectly certain that you can do so without risk to yourself, and never be in too great a hurry to inflict a lot of punishment early on. You want to make your opponent *beat himself*, and your surest way of doing that is to make him come at you and keep coming at you - hard.

Study him carefully. Never allow him to slacken. If he does pull up, be very sure about his reason for doing so. Avoid being led into any trap. He may have pulled up to get you to come to him, or he may have done so for the sake of a much-needed breather. In either case, be careful that you don't hesitate.

You will, I assume, have taken particular pains to study this man and his methods beforehand. That is unless you are a thoroughly experienced ring-craftsman and are well able to sum up almost any situation at a glance.

In either case it is as well to get in on to him quickly. Should you find it necessary to feint in order to draw him for an opening, be sure to keep an extra wary eye open for a heavy punch, since these sloggers have practised the art of hitting out fiercely and dangerously from the most unlikely positions and attitudes. Get in, if you can, and sting him severely when you do get in. For choice select his nose as your target and rap it smartly. Don't tap it. Remember that there are few things which are so calculated to annoy or irritate a man as a really sharp rap on the nose. Then, if he refuses to rush, step in and give him another reminder on the same place.

This is, of course, assuming that your path thereto is open. It may very possibly not be if the other fellow happens to be the true rough slogger, because the main idea of defence possessed by these gentry is a smother of their features by both arms, which, accompanied by a crouching attitude, renders them by no means easy to hit. I have explained elsewhere [in the book *The Text Book of Boxing*] several useful methods of breaking up even some of the closest smothers, and either of these may be selected according to the circumstances of the case. But due caution should be always observed in doing so, because these fellows have a wonderfully smart knack of lashing out straight away with scarcely any warning. So it is as well to be always prepared to either leap or sway back into safety at the first sign of an attack.

Should you decide that the risk isn't worth it, you may be content to administer the push sideways, followed by a rib drive and possibly the rabbit punch to the back of the neck. You may even find it possible to dodge round your man and to hand him quite a number of rabbit punches. These will not count anything towards your score, but they will annoy him and will also help to weaken him more than a trifle.

On the other hand, should he open out to meet you, you

THE DRAW

The draw for the left lead to the face to gain an opening for a left body counter.

will find your troubles considerably lightened. For he will in that case assuredly attempt to "get you" with a mighty swing. In that case it is open to your own judgment whether you dart in and out again before he can let go, or whether you elect to slip right in with a drive to the nose and perhaps a right-hander to the body, ducking as you do so and allowing the swing to encircle your neck. But in any case, when you have so stepped in, be very careful to prevent his getting to work at in-fighting. You have or should have taken the interior lines by storm and should consequently be able to keep both arms out of action until you are ordered to break away, when you must spring back, if you can, well clear of him, paying special heed to the danger of receiving a particularly awkward punch as you do break away.

In any case you have got to get clear and in any case it is your plain duty to send home another nose-ender as soon as possible. For you simply must get him off on the chase again.

You want to coax him to pursue you, at full pelt, and you want to keep him doing so. The more frequently he charges, and the more furiously he does so, the sooner is his wind going to go. Should you deem it advisable to do so, you will find it distinctly profitable to lay a few traps for him: up against the ropes, say, or in your own or a neutral corner (preferably not in his own, because you may not be over anxious for him to receive any valuable advice from his seconds just then). The traps will of course be baited by yourself. You will so place yourself as to convey the impression that you are cornered and cannot escape, with the further impression that you are most anxious to do so. This will in most cases bring him charging at you furiously, and in that case it is always as well to be certain of your avenue of escape. Since he will usually come swinging at you, by the way, this should not be so very difficult to find, for you can always duck under his arms and away to the centre of the ring.

It seems to me that you have it there, or at least all of it you will want to have. You have got to keep this fellow on the

Georges Carpentier beating an opponent to the punch by drawing back from the body lead and sending his own right to the face.

move, and to rely chiefly on your left hand. Never or hardly ever chance anything with your right, unless you are practically certain of getting home with it, and get and keep away and around as much as you can.

Don't be too sure that you have exhausted him. When you hear him blowing and see that he is in distress, use every wile and every lure of which you can think to make him come after you again. Try and make him go faster than ever before. Slip him more narrowly. Worry him and infuriate him as much as you can - and above all don't neglect his nose. The more frequently you rap that, the earlier you are going to win; because every time you rap it you are going to increase his annoyance and his fury, and at the same time to swell the tide of blood down his throat. A further trouble to his breathing, this.

You will know when the final stages of exhaustion are arriving quite soon enough. You will be able to tell it by his laboured breathing, by his gait, and most surely of all, in the clinches by the *feel* of his arms. Don't let him rest. It is to be hoped that you will yourself be in really excellent trim, because this is going to be a wearing bout for both of you. Keep him at it faster than ever as soon as he starts to weaken in reality. On no account allow him to get his second wind, and then when you have him really tired and really wobbling, go in and finish him.

But when the time arrives do your very best to make it as artistic a finish as you can. For if you have the artistic ideal before you, you will be less liable to make the mistake of hurrying over it. I have seen any number of contests, and I daresay you have also seen any number more, which have been simply chucked away by men who had their opponents beat to the world, but who were in such a feverish haste to finish them off, that they actually not only gave them time to recover; but absolutely placed themselves right into the very path of a punch which, for all that it may have been a decidedly lucky one, managed to completely turn the tables.

Jimmy Wilde's side-step. Pushing an opponent's left aside and jabbing his own left to the body.

CHAPTER FOUR
THE WALKING-IN OR STAND-UP OPPONENT

We have already dealt with the opponent who comes at you in a whirlwind of wrath. The man who tries to carry a thunderbolt in each hand and whose every effort is devoted to the hope of wiping you off the face of the earth.

A more awkward, if in some respects less dangerous, man (for the simple reason that he can be calculated more exactly) is the man who marches up to you, who refuses to rush or to be coaxed out of his stride, and who yet carries a real knock-out wallop in either hand, and who is above all going to make you wish you had never taken up the boxing game as a profession if ever you allow him to get to close quarters with you.

On the whole, as will be readily understood, this man is going to give you ever so much more trouble to beat. He is, emphatically, not one of those men you can ever coax into beating himself. He may be a fine boxer as well as a strong and rugged fighter. He may be deeply experienced in all the wiles and tricks of the trade, and he may know quite as much of the game as you do. How are you going to beat this man? Say that he is physically stronger, perhaps younger and more vigorous, possibly endowed by Nature with a harder punch and a greater appetite for punishment. He will surely prove a distinctly hard nut to crack. But if you are a really sound and well-cultivated out-fighter your task should not prove to be of any insuperable difficulty - that is, supposing that you have a really good punch of your own, an accurate and hard-hitting left (don't forget to cultivate that left-hand punch, if you have not done so already) and have really seriously and conscientiously developed your footwork to as near perfection as you could contrive.

In practising for this style of opponent, it is a good plan to develop your timing as much as possible. Work up your speed and the rapidity with which you hit out. Get your sparring partners to start a punch at you and then let go yourself and beat them to it - that is to say, endeavour to get home before they can, in spite of having given them that fraction of

SIDE-STEPPING A LEFT LEAD

Side-stepping a left lead and sending right to the jaw as your opponent goes past.

a second's start.

Another useful punch to have in your locker is the double punch, either with left or right or as a swiftly repeated shot for the hand which first arrives. You will find both very useful if you succeed in drawing your opponent at all frequently, but don't adhere to anyone method, and above all, against this type of adversary always be particularly chary of using your right hand. In fact, it is generally advisable to refrain from using the right at all, unless you are practically certain of landing, or have the knack of changing your feet smartly and can consequently lead with your right as a left, and bring the left over as a right.

This last isn't half a bad move to employ against a man who makes a regular practice of moving round to your left in order to avoid the danger of running on to your right hand, since by a swift change of feet at the precisely right moment you may perhaps trick him into running on to your left hand (used as a right instead).

There is a general consensus of agreement that it is an unsound policy to lead off with the right especially at the body, but I have frequently done it with success and have been told that in my last fight with Owen Moran, actually the last time I ever appeared in serious contest, I not only led off with my right but did so repeatedly and frequently with both success and effect, particularly during the

Owen Moran

earlier rounds. The fact is, there are really very few hard-and-fast rules to be laid down about the practice of boxing. There are quite a number of things which it is inadvisable to attempt, and yet pretty nearly each and everyone of these things may be done with both success and effect on occasion. So much will depend on circumstances. For in boxing, perhaps more than in anything else, nothing succeeds so well as the unexpected. I might even go further and say with perfect truth that nothing succeeds *save* the unexpected.

Don't try to uppercut too frequently. The uppercut is a most useful blow and usually effective when it lands, but a man may use it too freely, particularly if that man has seen a good deal of Packey McFarland and has a leaning towards his style. For Packey relies more extensively on the right uppercut, perhaps, than any other boxer of recent years, and it is really astonishing that he should have escaped serious injury to his hand through this pet habit of his. For that is the real danger of the uppercut. It is so easy to bring it into violent contact with an interposed elbow, in which case it may be put out of action for the rest of the contest.

Packey McFarland

But to return to our imaginary opponent and to the most effective and useful method of dealing with him. We have said that this man is disinclined to rush. Well, in that case you must coax him into rushing, to the very best of your ability. In the first place you will naturally want to disturb his balance as much as you are able, and there is nothing which tends to throw a man off his balance and out of his stride so readily as a sudden rush or charge, particularly if the said dash forward is rendered abortive. And if the man is unused to attacks of this nature he will be the more readily unbalanced, particularly if he comes in with a swinging attack. Those swings will be dangerous of course - all swings are. But then, since they are swings and not straight punches, they mayor should be avoided with comparative ease. You can duck or step inside to deliver a sharp jab, or you can step back out of the way to allow him to lose his balance, which loss you can assist con-

Johnny Kilbane delivering an uppercut to an opponent

siderably by a judicious tap on his arm as it passes you.

In a somewhat similar fashion, you will find it a very useful practice to side-step or retreat just an inch or so out of the way of a straight left lead and then push it sharply with your own left as it shoots past. In that case you will have naturally stepped off to the right with your right foot and will be standing practically at right angles to him, with his jaw beautifully exposed to a jab from your left or a smash from your right. Even if you have stepped too far to your right front or he has advanced farther than you anticipated, you are very well placed to plant your right behind his ear.

We have already supposed him to be a smart and clever in-fighter, and in that case you will naturally wish to avoid any in-fighting if you can possibly contrive to do so. Yet, as this is almost certain to be forced on you, or rather as he will almost certainly make a big effort to get to close quarters, it is just as well to be fully prepared for all emergencies.

In fact, if you feel that you can step in close or can welcome him to that position with a reasonable certainty that you will be able to secure the inside position -that is to say, with both your arms inside his - don't hesitate to take the chance.

You may then block any attempts on his part to hit you with either hand, since you can force these wide on either side with your own forearms or gloves, and can, from that position, without even the semblance of holding or clinching, whip in any number of swift jabs to his face, chin and body. He will be, at all events for several seconds (if you play your moves correctly), powerless alike for offence or defence, so that you will, be able to rattle up quite a decent tally of points and perhaps may even be able to inflict some quite serious punishment, before you judge it advisable to step clear again and leave him to reflect on the possibility that he is by no means the great all-conquering in-fighter he fondly believed himself to be.

A few repetitions of this sort of thing will almost certainly either disabuse his mind altogether of the belief that he is

THE RABBIT PUNCH

The Rabbit Punch applied to an opponent whom you have slipped.

really and truly a master at this department, or, even if it fails to have quite that effect, you will have at least considerably weakened his faith in himself. He may then essay either to beat you at long-range boxing or he may display his prowess as a rushing two-handed fighter, and in either of those cases his downfall should not be long delayed. For once let a man start out to do something to which he is unaccustomed and you should have him at your mercy, comparatively speaking. He is not playing his own game. You have got him guessing, and you will have forced him to change his methods by instilling in his mind the conviction that you are a better man than he is in the very department in which he was convinced (before the fight commenced) that he was going to prove your master.

He may, perhaps, have believed, or rather may have hoped, that he was going to beat you in several other branches of the game as well. But whatever he may have fancied about his chances at boxing you for points, purely and simply, and however he may have esteemed his likely fortune as a furious two-handed aggressive fighter, it is practically certain that he failed to include you in his in-fighting calculations at all.

You have no particular reputation in that branch. You are known perhaps either as a moderately skilled, or a really skilled, long-range boxer, and he has not, consequently, worried himself about anything you might be able to do at close quarters. And it was for this reason that he did his best to get you mixed up in a *corps á corps* exchange. He was puzzled at first that you should have more or less welcomed his invitation, for at all events you certainly did not decline it. Why? He knows now. He, the pastmaster at in-fighting, has actually been beaten at his own game. It is true that he has had the worst of the few in-fighting spells simply because he has been *out-fought* at them (in a double sense). But this explanation may not have readily occurred to him. The bald fact that he has had the worst of matters is plain and obvious in

Out-Fighting: The Deluxe Edition • 57

Carpentier side-steps and right hooks the face.

Bombardier Billy Wells, English boxer, preparing in Rye, New York, for fight with Al Palzer.

all its hideousness, and its grim aspect may well have dwarfed every other vision.

For which good and sufficient reasons he will in all probability come at you in either of the other two guises which he may select with a considerably dampened confidence. He will be uncertain, even doubtful, of his own powers and more than probably decidedly apprehensive of yours. In which case you should find him a more or less easy victim. Your speedier footwork will now come doubly to your aid, for you should not find it either particularly difficult to draw him, nor overwhelmingly difficult to avoid him, while you will be able to get home more of your pet blows than you have usually found yourself able to do in serious contests.

He will be worried with himself. He may even be both

annoyed and disgusted with himself. He will be irritated with you and furiously anxious to pay back some of his past humiliations with interest. And this, from every point of view, is about as agreeable a state of affairs from your standpoint as you could possibly desire.

CHAPTER FIVE
SOME IMPORTANT POINTS TO BE OBSERVED

At the out-fighting game, more than in any other department, it is most advisable to be careful always to punch with the knuckle part of the gloves. In the first place, because there are so many opportunities for flicking with them. In the second, because whereas a flick or slap may frequently pass muster as a genuine punch, even under a moderately conscientious referee, in an in-fighting exchange or close rally; it stands a much smaller chance of being credited at anything more than its intrinsic worth at long range, where it can be so readily seen to be just exactly what it is. And thirdly and lastly, since you are boxing at long range and are open to give and take, you really cannot afford to waste even a fractional part of the value of any single punch.

Then - and I would like you all to pay very particular attention indeed to this, since it is a point of really the very first importance - NEVER on any account permit yourselves to fall into the most lamentable error of pushing with the open or closed glove. These feeble and almost inane dabs and pushes, especially with the left glove, have been responsible for more British defeats than anything else our men have ever done or left undone. A most pernicious and at the same time a most extraordinary superstition would seem to have grown up among our latter-day professionals, which founds itself on the idea that the left hand is a weapon with which more or less feeble points may be scored, while the right hand is alone to be regarded as the punching or punishing member. How this idea originated, or where, or by whom it was first preached, no one seems to know. All that any of us do know about it is that it is most lamentably prevalent and has remained so, despite the long list of defeats at the hands of foreign and home rivals which it has brought in its train.

To a very considerable degree our referees are largely responsible for its continued existence, or at all events for its existence in one of its very worst phases. They have allowed boxers of every degree, from champions down to novices, to flick and push with an open and fully extended left glove,

ENGLISH BOXERS SHOW UP STRONGLY

Only One Britisher Fails to Outpoint His Opponent in Special Tournament

New York Times
May 28, 1911

The five English boxers who recently came to this country to compete in the international boxing tournament were given their tryouts last night in some special matches against the pick of American amateurs at the National Sporting Club, and easily showed themselves superior to the home talent. Metropolitan, National, and Canadian champions competed in the exhibitions, but none showed up to advantage, as did the Englishmen. They were awarded three of the five bouts in which they took part, and the decision which deprived W. W. Allen, the 115-pound boy, the honors over Tommy Regan of Boston was greeted with catcalls, jeers, and hisses. Allen clearly outpointed his opponent, and the ovation which the crowd tendered him as he left the ring

without once disqualifying them and with only a few occasional calls to order. Well, perhaps a few men have been disqualified, but these have been very few in number, while I have seen several champions and any number of near champions practise it with impunity and without even a warning, a reprimand, or a reminder that an open glove push can by no possibility qualify as a pointearner.

One need, surely, only ask the guilty boxers themselves, the referees who have indulged them, and the spectators who have ignorantly applauded them, how they would fare if their hands were not protected by gloves, to prove to them that they had been extremely lucky to escape the disqualifications they have. The practice is trebly objectionable. Firstly, because it is against the rules; secondly, because it is an unfair attempt to steal points from an incompetent or near-sighted referee by meanly adding an unjustifiable inch or so to the length of the reach; and thirdly and principally, because the practice has done more harm to the repute of British long-range boxing than anything else of which one can think at the moment.

How on earth does any man imagine that he is going to check the onslaught of any strong or determined opponent by a gentle open-glove push of this description? It is true, if the push lands fairly frequently in the neighbourhood of the eyes or on the nose, for example, that it may have both visible and painful effects. But it is never going to stop or even to check a strong determined man from coming in close. Does anyone wonder that the Frenchmen and the Americans laugh at our adherence to our old and well-tried straight left, when this is the sort of counterfeit to which they are introduced with the assurance that it is the genuine article. But the worst result remains to be told.

This open-glove left push has infected British boxing everywhere. The vast majority of our left-hand exponents today appear to be quite satisfied so long as they can land a series of feeble left-hand pushes. They rarely attempt to must have made up for the decision which had been denied.

There was one exception to the general run of English speed. This was in the case of Frank Parks, who claims to have won the amateur heavyweight championship of England five times. He faced William Spengler, the metropolitan title holder, in the final number of the evening, and his work was a big disappointment. He showed no marks of a champion at any stage, and was clearly outpointed the New York boy.

The star of the lot was Ralph Erskine, the seventeen-year-old boy who fights in the 125-pound class. He fought Alfred Roffe, the Canadian champion, and simply toyed with his opponent all through the three rounds. He had all the actions of an experienced performer, and the speed of a Jem Driscoll. He easily outpointed Roffe.

R. C. Warner, the English middleweight, showed a terrific left punch in his bout with Nap Boutillier, the National champion at that weight, and at the close of the three rounds there was no question about the verdict, Warner winning by a good margin.

The opening bout brought together two 125-pounders, Tommy Regan of Boston and W. W. Allen of England. Regan started well, but Allen came back strong in the third round. The judges disagreed on a decision, and an extra round was ordered. At the end of the extra period the judges still disagreed, and Referee Haley gave his decision in favor of Regan. The verdict proved decidedly unpopular and was greeted with hisses. There were a few cheers for Regan as he crossed the ring to shake hands with Allen, but they stopped abruptly when Regan collapsed in his corner, Allen was loudly cheered as he left the ring.

Alfred Spenceley, England's 135-pound champion, found a difficult opponent in Tom McGovern of the New West Side Athletic Club. The Briton was a much better boxer, but McGovern was built on more rugged lines, could take the punishment, and had a harder punch. Spenceley's jabbing and clever defensive work kept him in the lead in the second and third rounds, and there was no question about the verdict. Spenceley was floored early in the first round, but he came back strong and floored McGovern twice before the end of the bout.

do anything else, save when, dissatisfied with the progress they are making towards a knockout, they pick up their right hand and send it over more or less on a chance errand, in the desperate hope that *that* at least will do some real damage.

Strange to say, the futility and utter uselessness of the whole procedure has scarcely been noticed here at home. Our men walk into a ring, stroll round each other and shape up. One of them threatens an attack. The other languidly places a gentle left hand somewhere on his would-be assailant's face and that gentleman at once pulls back and begins to work up to something else.

The gentle tapper seems to feel that he has done everything which was required of him. He has scored with a straight left and will in all probability now attempt to score with another one or two, while the recipient will dodge around, retreat in despair, and tell his friends afterwards that the other fellow's left hand was far too good for him and that he could find no way of getting

THE BILLY PAPKE VERSUS JIM SULLIVAN CONTEST FOR THE WORLD'S MIDDLEWEIGHT CHAMPIONSHIP

Here was a striking illustration of the futility of the modern English left hand. Sullivan's left was rarely out of Papke's face, but the American was unhurt and was able to walk right into Sullivan in the eighth round and beat him with a single drive to the body. As will be noticed, Sullivan's left punch was usually an open-gloved affair.

round it. Perhaps it was too accurate to get *round*, but surely it wasn't so forcible that he couldn't walk through it! The press and the critics omit to notice this latter point and so promptly go into ecstasies of joy. "At long last," they tell us,

SECURING THE INTERIOR LINES

Securing the interior lines and thereby preventing your opponent from hitting you with either hand.

"Great Britain has unearthed a most worthy champion who will show these foreigners a thing or two and who will speedily restore our ancient prestige." They wax so enthusiastic about him and his doings that we who have never had the misfortune to see him, journey perhaps hundreds of miles to watch him uphold the honour of the country against a foreign invader. And all we see or are able to see is the long, feeble, spineless, left push, which the invader either contemptuously brushes to one side, when he doesn't scornfully force his way past it, to march right in to close quarters and fell our great champion with a couple or so of punches, which he has neither the wit, the stamina nor the footwork to avoid.

No; if we want to regain the world's or even the European titles in the heavier divisions, the welters, the middles and the heavies - and, for that matter, the bantams - we must see to it that our men begin to learn the rudiments of the English style. They must learn how to move around, they must learn how to adapt themselves to circumstances, they must set themselves seriously to train on the right lines and in the right spirit, and, above all, they must learn how to *punch*, swiftly, accurately and *straight* from short or long range, with either hand and with the clenched fist. In short, they must start to learn out-fighting which so many of them fondly (but foolishly imagine that they) know already.

ADDENDUM

JEM DRISCOLL BEATS BALDWIN

English Boxer Scores Easy Victory Over Boston Man at Fairmont Athletic Club

New York Times
November 14, 1908

Jem Driscoll, the English featherweight champion, made his American debut last night at the Fairmont Athletic Club, where he outpointed Matty Baldwin of Boston in a six-round bout. Driscoll showed himself to be a shifty two-handed boxer and held the upper hand throughout the bout. His style is much on the order of Palmer and Plimmer, when those two fighters were in their prime, but he lacked their cleverness, although he may appear to better advantage when he becomes accustomed to the surroundings. He was somewhat nervous during the early part of the first round, but when once settled down, he showed himself to be a clever boxer and master of many of the tricks of the ring.

Owing to the unsettled conditions regarding the boxing game, there was only a fair attendance, but those who risked the possibility of police interference were rewarded by witnessing an interesting contest. Baldwin, always somewhat slow and deliberate, was exasperatingly so throughout the six rounds, and only once did he make any pretense of meeting the Britisher on even ground. This was in the fifth round, when the Bostonian, after being jabbed repeatedly, began to fight back. He rushed Driscoll, and although he did not land many blows, he kept his opponent on the defensive, and for this round made matters even.

After recovering his nervousness in the initial round, Driscoll caught his man flush in the face with a straight right punch, which caused the blood to flow freely. He kept up his good work, jabbing Baldwin frequently in the face and occasionally visiting the body with right swings. The Boston fighter was forced to cover up in the second round, as Driscoll drove him all over the ring. Baldwin appeared very tired at the end of the round.

The third and fourth rounds were repetitions of the earlier ones, and Driscoll always held the upper hand. Baldwin could not reach the shifty Britisher. A fast exchange opened the sixth round, but Driscoll was all over his man and reached his head with hard right swings. Baldwin was very tired as he went to his corner at the end of the fight.

Remembering Jem Driscoll

by Bohun Lynch
Boxing Correspondent
Field and Sport

From the spectator's point of view much of the interest of boxing (and almost all of it in amateur boxing), is purely dramatic. You can thoroughly enjoy - at least I can, and there are others - a really good fight apart from any science that may be displayed. For enjoyment of skill alone is in another dimension. Of course, there must always be enough science to enable the boxers to fight cleanly and tidily and without the appearance of two angry windmills. But greatly as science improves the complete interest and enjoyment of a fight, that kind of interest remains separate. For the admiration of skill appeals to your head, the drama, largely to your heart. And the drama in boxing arises from the fact that the encounter is a personal one, that two men are trying to hurt each other, at least physically to overcome each other (which amounts to the same thing) and to prevent the other from hurting, from dominating. There is no other sport in which the sense of personal combat is so manifest.

And it is partly because of this dramatic interest that heavyweights - big men - have, as a rule, throughout two hundred years, attracted greater attention than the little men, except, of course, when little men have fought with big ones. Roughly, it is like this: if you want to see scientific boxing you choose a fight between feather or bantamweights, if you want to see a good slogging match (but tempered with science, always) you choose a fight between middle or heavyweights, preferably the latter.

I should like to have described the fights of many of the lesser men in point of size - far better boxers, most of them, than almost any heavyweight that ever lived. Names topple out of recent memory at random - Billy Plimmer, Pedlar Palmer, Joe Bowker, Charles Ledoux, Johnny Summers, Tancy Lee, Johnny Basham, hosts of them. But there is one name that simply cannot be avoided in any book about any sort of boxing, the name of one of the best featherweights and one of the fairest fighters that ever lived - Jem Driscoll.

Driscoll, who was formerly Featherweight Champion of England, having won the Lonsdale Belt outright by three successful contests, had all the natural gifts of the boxer. His weight was 9 stone, or, at all events, generally within easy reach of it; his height 5 feet 6 inches. He was beautifully proportioned, slim, muscular, with the appearance of an all-round athlete. His science was unrivalled, and he was a perfect exponent of what one may still call the English style of boxing; that is, the style based upon the upright position and the conspicuous use of the straight left lead. Driscoll is Irish by extraction and Welsh by birth, and he loved fighting for fighting's sake from his earliest childhood. He went in for and won various

boys' competitions at Cardiff, and, later, travelled with a booth; his only instructor being experience.

His two contests at the National Sporting Club with Spike Robson, of Newcastle, for the English Featherweight Belt, are worth a brief note in order to show Driscoll at the height of his power. Robson was three or four years older, but a very tough customer, with any amount of pluck. The first match, which took place on April 18th, 1910, had been keenly anticipated for a long time beforehand, if only because everything in which Driscoll had a hand was worth seeing. You always knew where you were with Driscoll. He always hit clean, and for choice, straight. There was never any clinching to avoid punishment, never any getting on the "blind side" of the referee.

The first three rounds were level. Robson was a good boxer, a keen fighter, but he was neither so quick with his hands or feet as Driscoll. However, it was he who landed the first considerable blow in the fourth round, striking heavily on his opponent's eye. In the fifth round he did a very foolish thing. There was something about his gay, elegant, upright and good-looking antagonist which irritated him. Driscoll was so indifferent, so imperturbable. He would smash him, he would spoil his face for him. The instant the bell rang for time he would catch Driscoll before he was clear of his corner, before, in fact, he was ready. That was the way to smash him - to give him no time to take up his position in the middle of the ring, with his left foot and arm out, nicely balanced on his toes. He'd show him. And he charged furiously head down across the ring like a terrier after his best enemy. And Jem Driscoll merely waited, until Robson was almost on him and then coolly stepped aside. It was beautifully done - no haste, no exertion, only the exactly right judgment of time. And Spike Robson couldn't recover himself - he was going much too fast for that - and was brought up by crashing into the stool which the seconds had not yet been able to remove from Driscoll's corner.

The edge of the stool cut his scalp severely as, from the fact that Robson was prematurely bald, was immediately obvious. He was half dazed, and had only sense for the rest of that round to clinch and lean on his opponent. The referee had to caution him severely for doing so. He had somewhat recovered in the next round, and in the seventh he was boxing well, though he had suffered a considerable shock. And Driscoll was boxing better, and would have been, I would venture to say, in any case and without the accident to handicap his antagonist. In the eleventh round Robson showed an inclination again to take a rest by leaning on his man in a clinch, and the referee observed with noticeable firmness: "Robson, I shall not tell you again." And when they were once more at long range Driscoll sent in six blows, one after another with lightning speed and almost without a return. Such blows as these may not have been each very hard, but their cumulative effect was fatiguing and depressing. Robson got a very warm time in the next two rounds; but he was thoroughly game, and kept on returning to the fight every time that Driscoll drove him away at the end of his long left. To the spectator who does not watch a fight of this kind, between two small men, with a very vigilant eye, the end often comes with surprising abruptness. In this case, Robson had been getting a much worse time than it seemed to any but the most careful observer. Driscoll had done as he liked with him latterly, and instead of his blows gradually losing power, in spite of the fact that he had a cold and was not in the best possible condition, they were all the harder because weariness in the other man had made them safer, the openings more patent. At the beginning of the fifteenth round, Driscoll sent in a sharp left hook, followed immediately with a right, and Robson tumbled forward to the floor. He rose very slowly, needing all his determination to do so, and as Driscoll sent him down again, the referee  stopped the fight. Robson was much more hurt than, until the last minute, he seemed: and it was some minutes before he fully recovered his senses.

The second encounter between these men, on January 30, 1911, was a much shorter affair. Driscoll on this occasion was in perfect condition, and he knew the worst of Robson. To begin with, he boxed with extraordinary speed, and though his blows were light, they were many. There was an admirable example of his powers in the second round, for he sent over a right hook with great power, which Robson dodged, and which, had it been struck by a clumsier boxer, would certainly have left him clean open to a counter; but when Robson's counter came in, as it did with commendable speed, Driscoll's right was back in its place to guard it. Beyond that failure, Driscoll made no effort to knock his man out until the fifth round. He contented himself with left, left, left, not very hard but very wearing. Then in the fifth round he became a fighter again: and before Robson knew he was there he fell before a right-hander on the point of the jaw. Through the sixth round

Driscoll, who never who never took a situation for granted and ever remained careful until he had been proclaimed the winner, boxed hard, but gave no chances. Left, right - left, right: his blows nearly all landed, and Robson's blows were growing feeble and wild. In the seventh round he was palpably done, and Driscoll hit him as he liked, finally sending him down for six seconds. In the next round the referee decided that Robson had been hit enough. Towards the end Driscoll had been holding back and trying not to hurt his opponent. And that was Driscoll "all over."

In writing of Driscoll, it is fitting that an international contest of his should be described in which he was matched against the Featherweight Champion of France, Jean Poesy. This fight took place towards the end of Driscoll's career, on June 3rd, 1912, at the National Sporting Club. In his quiet way, Driscoll was confident of beating Poesy. They had seen each other, though not in the ring, but the English fancied his own chances merely from the "cut of his jib." They were equal in height and weight, but Driscoll had the advantage of long experience. True, he was over thirty, but before the fight he declared that he could hit as hard and stay as well as ever he could.

So they entered the ring - the young Frenchman and the veteran. As ever, Driscoll showed that he was the master of scientific fisticuffs: he was wonderfully quick, and he could still take hard knocks without showing a sign. Poesy was no novice: he could box well and was not so foolish as to underestimate his opponent, as many a young 'un would have done. He began on the defensive, so that Jem Driscoll had to carry the war into the enemy's country, and once more he showed he could outfight as well as outgeneral a good youth. There was never a question as to who would win, and in the end Driscoll left the ring without a mark, without having received a single damaging blow. All the same, it was an interesting fight, because of Poesy's pluck and the English champion's really amazing skill, which showed no falling off from his old high standard. He kept Poesy at long range, never leaving an opening for a knockout blow, which the Frenchman soon saw was his only chance; never clinching or hugging. It is a pity that more men did not profit by his exam-

ple. Poesy tried to get at Driscoll's body. He had beaten Digger Stanley like that. But Driscoll understood in-fighting too, though for choice he boxed at long range. In the tenth and eleventh rounds Poesy woke up and fought like a little fiend. Some one called out from the crowd, "When Poesy does take it into his head to get a move on, you'll see something." But all the spectators saw was a ferocious, game, and persevering attack coolly frustrated; and the more the Frenchman attacked, the more he left himself open, so that Driscoll was now hitting harder and oftener than before. Poesy was in beautiful condition, and began the twelfth round with unabated ardour. He dashed at Driscoll and landed a really hard straight left on his jaw. That made Driscoll think for a moment, and he decided that it would not be well to risk too many of that sort. Almost immediately afterwards Poesy coming in, left himself open, and Driscoll knocked him clean off his feet with a right on the chin. The Frenchman gallantly struggled up in five seconds, obviously dazed. Driscoll feinted and dodged about this way and that, so that it was impossible to tell whence the next blow would come, and presently sent over another right which knocked Poesy out of time . . . eight, nine, ten! Then Driscoll bent down and picked him up and carried him to his corner. Not at any weight nor at any time was the Championship of England held by a better boxer or a straighter man.

AVAILABLE NOW

Scientific Boxing: The Deluxe Edition
by James J. Corbett

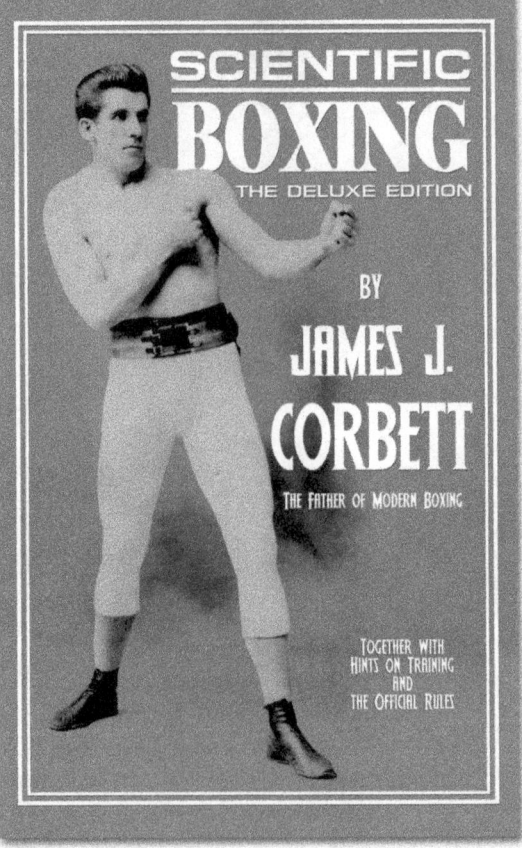

In 1892, "Gentleman" James J. Corbett defeated John L. Sullivan to become the heavyweight champion of the world. Using his own "scientific boxing" techniques, Corbett delivered a blistering lesson to the previously unbeatable Sullivan, ending the fight with a knockout in the 21st round. With Corbett's win, a new era in boxing began.

Corbett is considered by many to be the "father of modern boxing" for being the first person to apply scientific principles to the art of pugilism. In *Scientific Boxing*, the creator of such boxing innovations as the "left hook" distills his scientific methodology into an accessible manual of boxing techniques. This classic book contains sections on fundamental boxing techniques, fouling techniques, and the various boxing rules of his time.

This deluxe edition of *Scientific Boxing* contains additional photos and an added account of the fight between Corbett and Sullivan.

ISBN 978-0-9737698-9-0
WWW.PROMETHEAN-PRESS.COM

ADDITIONAL TITLES IN THIS SERIES:

Out-Fighting by Jim Driscoll
The Straight Left by Jim Driscoll
The Text Book of Boxing by Jim Driscoll
Ringcraft by Jim Driscoll

www.ingramcontent.com/pod-product-compliance
Lightning Source LLC
Chambersburg PA
CBHW051948160426
43198CB00013B/2346